ALSO BY DAVID THOMSON

Showman:
The Life of David O. Selznick

Silver Light

Warren Beatty and Desert Eyes

Suspects

Overexposures

Scott's Men

America in the Dark

Wild Excursions:
The Life and Fiction of Laurence Sterne

Hungry as Hunters

A Bowl of Eggs

Movie Man